# COMPLICATED RELATIONSHIP

*How to deal with it whether new or old romance*

***SAMSON ABLE***

Table of contents

REASONS FOR COMPLICATED RELATIONSHIPS

## CHAPTER THREE

TRY TO END THE COMPLICATION

TALK TO YOUR PARTNER

## CHAPTER FOUR

COMPLICATED RELATIONSHIPS THAT JUST CAN'T WORK

ARE YOU READY FOR A FRESH START?

# CHAPTER FIVE

## CONCLUSION

# INTRODUCTION

The perfect relationship can quickly become complicated, and no lover can truly predict it without listening to the other's turmoil. But in almost all cases, complicated relationships are one-sided love affairs where one person wants to hold on while the other wants to let go or go with someone else.

# CHAPTER ONE

*So are you in a complicated relationship?*

It's easy to understand how to navigate complex relationships when you can see the facts clearly.

*Why are your relationships so complicated at all?*

Learning to see problems in clear light is the first step in solving relationship problems. Most of the time, people in complicated relationships don't realize their problems because they're either not interested in acknowledging them, or they're too emotionally clouded to accept reality.

# CHAPTER TWO

## *Deal with complicated relationships*

Complicated relationship status on Facebook might seem like a cool thing to show off, but a complicated relationship can be a great time to be alone and question what's really going on in your love life. It's heartbreaking and painful to experience when you're thinking about it.

### *Reasons for complicated relationships*

Complex relationships can arise for a variety of reasons, ranging from falling in love, falling in love with someone else, bitter arguments, and sharp remarks, to confusing issues such as bedmates and relationships where one uses the other. There is a possibility. If you are on the receiving end of a complicated relationship, don't try to resolve the complications just yet. Instead, think about what really bothers you and how you intend to deal with it. Complicated relationships almost always don't have happy endings, especially if the love is one-sided. And

when you think of a
crush, it's definitely not a
complicated relationship.
It's just a crush.

# CHAPTER THREE

## *Try to end the complication*

The complexity of relationships has never been the same. So you have to find your own way of manipulating it to offset the complexity. Complications can occur in long-term relationships when your partner falls in love with someone else or loses interest in you as a potential partner. There are times when the novelty of a new relationship wears off, or your date simply doesn't want to date you for a variety of reasons. So what are you going to do about it?

### *Talk to your partner*

The easiest way to resolve a complicated relationship is to talk it over with your partner.

You may find it easier to live in denial and avoid facing situations. But even if it means talking to your partner at the cost of losing the relationship or ending it altogether, do it... talk to your partner. In the most complicated relationships, the partner may be too timid to end the relationship and may want to avoid the partner for tips. You may be happily trying to handle a complicated relationship situation, but your partner may be with someone else. When you're stuck in a complicated relationship, find the strength to face it, no matter how painful it is to face it. You can at least know what is happening.

# CHAPTER FOUR

## *Complicated relationships that just can't work*

If you find yourself in a relationship where your partner cheats on you all the time or says he doesn't want to be with you anymore but sometimes comes back into your arms or your partner ignores you, if so, it's a clear sign that the relationship is going nowhere. Your partner may be just trying to find someone else, or he may take advantage of you until he finds someone else. Or they may be too timid to break up with you. If talking and reassurance can't end the complication, chances are you two aren't separated.

## *Are you ready for a fresh start?*

Sometimes it's easier to just end the relationship and walk away, especially if there are too many complications. But if you really love your partner and want to get back together, take the chance. But we must remember that complex relationships rarely work out. If you're stuck at the painful ending of a complicated relationship, it means your partner is taking advantage of you, or being too selfish to care about anyone but yourself. Get out of complicated relationships if you can't work through your differences to resolve complex issues. It may hurt for a while, but no matter how much it hurts, nothing hurts more than it feels right now every day in a complicated life. You can remove it. Love sickness always heals with time, but complications only increase with time. Please remember this.

# CHAPTER FIVE

## *Conclusion*

Still want to know how to handle complex relationships? But you already know what to do, right? No matter how unique your complications are, there is only one way to clear them all. Confront it.

www.ingramcontent.com/pod-product-compliance
Lightning Source LLC
LaVergne TN
LVHW020546160826
845677LV00015B/4235

* 9 7 9 8 3 5 1 1 6 0 0 3 0 *